The
WORKING FROM HOME
Little Book Of
CALM

David Smythe

INTRODUCTION

THE PERFECT GIFT FOR FAMILY, FRIENDS & COWORKERS!

Are you or do you know someone who has been working from home recently?

Working from home can be great in many ways, but there are times when it can become a little challenging and stressful for everyone. All of us would like to have a little more calm in our lives when working from home, but how do we achieve this?

THE ANSWER?

The
WORKING FROM HOME
Little Book Of
CALM

This little book of inspirational quotations holds within it the timeless secrets of how all of us can achieve more calmness in our lives from the world's greatest thinkers of all time, from over 2000 years of human thought.

Read this little book and live with
more *CALM* today!

Enjoy!
David Smythe

"Anger dwells only in the bosom of fools."

ALBERT EINSTEIN

German-born theoretical physicist who developed the theory of relativity.

1979 - 1955

"Experience is not what happens to you - it's how you interpret what happens to you."

ALDOUS HUXLEY

English writer and philosopher.

1894 - 1963

> *"Control yourself or someone else will control you."*

UNKNOWN

"*Anyone can be angry – that is easy. But to be angry with the right person, to the right degree, at the right time, for the right purpose, and in the right way--that is not easy*".

ARISTOTLE

Greek philosopher and polymath during the Classical period in Ancient Greece.

384 BC - 344 BC

"I count him braver who overcomes his desires than him who conquers his enemies; for the hardest victory is over self."

ARISTOTLE

Greek philosopher and polymath during the
Classical period in Ancient Greece.

384 BC - 344 BC

"Never do anything when you are in a temper, for you will do everything wrong."

BALTASAR GRACIAN

Spanish Jesuit and baroque prose writer and philosopher.

1601 - 1658

"Empty your mind, be formless, shapeless, like water."

BRUCE LEE

Hong Kong-American actor, martial arts
instructor, and philosopher

1940 -1973

"In a controversy the instant we feel anger we have already ceased striving for the truth and have begun striving for ourselves."

BUDDHA

Philosopher, teacher and religious leader on whose teachings Buddhism was founded.

563 BC - 483 BC

"Those who are free of resentful thoughts surely find peace."

BUDDHA

Philosopher, teacher and religious leader on whose teachings Buddhism was founded.

563 BC - 483 BC

"When you realize how perfect everything is you will tilt your head back and laugh at the sky."

BUDDHA

Sage and philosopher on whose teachings Buddhism was founded.

Circa 6th or 4th centuries BC

"The most intense conflicts, if overcome, leave behind a sense of security and calm that is not easily disturbed. It is just these intense conflicts and their conflagration which are needed to produce valuable and lasting results."

CARL JUNG

Carl Gustav Jung was a Swiss psychiatrist and psychoanalyst who founded analytical psychology.

1875 - 1961

"The highest possible stage in moral culture is when we recognize that we ought to control our thoughts."

CHARLES DARWIN

English naturalist, geologist and biologist, best known for his contributions to the science of evolution

1809 - 1882

"Nothing is permanent in this wicked world — not even our troubles."

CHARLIE CHAPLIN

English comic actor, filmmaker, and composer.

1889 - 1977

"When the heart is at peace, "for" and "against" are forgotten."

CHUANG TZU

Chinese philosopher.

Circa 4th century BC

"The pursuit, even of the best things, ought to be calm and tranquil."

CICERO

Roman statesman, orator, lawyer and philosopher.

79 BC – 51 BC

"Life is really simple, but we insist on making it complicated."

CONFUCIUS

Chinese philosopher and politician.

551 BC - 479 BC

"Choose to be optimistic. It feels better."

DALAI LAMA

Spiritual leader of the Tibetan people.

1935 -

"We can never obtain peace in the outer world until we make peace with ourselves."

DALAI LAMA

Spiritual leader of the Tibetan people.

1935 -

"Do not let the behavior of others destroy your inner peace."

DALAI LAMA

Spiritual leader of the Tibetan people.

1935 -

"Men are disturbed not by things, but by the view which they take of them."

EPICTETUS

Greek Stoic philosopher.

Circa 55 – 135 AD

"Don't hope that events will turn out the way you want, welcome events in whichever way they happen: this is the path to peace."

EPICTETUS

Greek Stoic philosopher.

Circa 55 – 135 AD

"Happiness and freedom begin with a clear understanding of one principle. Some things are within your control. And some things are not."

EPICTETUS

Greek Stoic philosopher.

Circa 55 – 135 AD

"*When you are offended at any man's fault, turn to yourself and study your own failings. Then you will forget your anger.*"

EPICTETUS

Greek Stoic philosopher.

Circa 55 – 135 AD

"Anger makes dull men witty, but it keeps them poor."

FRANCIS BACON

English philosopher and statesman.

1561 - 1626

"This is the first preparatory schooling of intellectuality. One must not respond immediately to a stimulus; one must acquire a command of the obstructing and isolating instincts."

FRIEDRICH NIETZSCHE

German philosopher, essayist, and cultural critic.

1844 - 1900

"*To learn to see- to accustom the eye to calmness, to patience, and to allow things to come up to it; to defer judgment, and to acquire the habit of approaching and grasping an individual case from all sides. This is the first preparatory schooling of intellectuality. One must not respond immediately to a stimulus; one must acquire a command of the obstructing and isolating instincts.*"

FRIEDRICH NIETZSCHE, TWILIGHT OF THE IDOLS

German philosopher, essayist, and cultural critic.

1844 - 1900

"Anger and intolerance are the enemies of correct understanding."

MAHATMA GANDHI

Anti-colonial nationalist and political ethicist, who employed nonviolent resistance.

1869 – 1948

"*People become attached to their burdens sometimes more than the burdens are attached to them.*"

GEORGE BERNARD SHAW

Irish playwright, critic, polemicist and political activist.

1856-1950

"Within you, there is a stillness and a sanctuary to which you can retreat at any time and be yourself."

HERMANN HESSE

German-born poet, novelist, and painter.

1877 – 1962

"Remember to keep the mind calm in difficult moments."

———————————————

HORACE

Roman lyric poet.

Circa 65 BC - 8 BC

"When the odds are hopeless, when all seems to be lost, then is the time to be calm, to make a show of authority – at least of indifference"

IAN FLEMING

British author, journalist and naval intelligence officer who is best known for his James Bond series of spy novels

1908 - 1964

"Self-control is strength. Right thought is mastery. Calmness is power."

JAMES ALLEN

British philosophical writer.

1864 - 1912

"The more tranquil a man becomes, the greater is his success, his influence, his power for good. Calmness of mind is one of the beautiful jewels of wisdom."

JAMES ALLEN

British philosophical writer.

1864 - 1912

"I will be calm. I will be mistress of myself."

JANE AUSTEN, SENSE AND SENSIBILITY

English writer.

1775–1817

"Everything is hard, before it is easy."

JOHANN WOLFGANG VON GOETHE

German writer and statesman.

1749 - 1832

"*He who reigns within himself, and rules passions, desires, and fears, is more than a king.*"

JOHN MILTON

English poet and intellectual.

1608 – 1674

"The best fighter is never angry."

LAO TZU

Chinese philosopher and writer.

6th-century BC

"Make your heart like a lake, with a calm, still surface, and great depths of kindness."

LAO TZU

Chinese philosopher and writer.

6th-century BC

"Mastering others is strength, mastering yourself is true power."

LAO TZU

Chinese philosopher and writer.

6th-century BC

"If you correct your mind, the rest of your life will fall into place."

LAO TZU

Chinese philosopher and writer.

6th-century BC

Care about what other people think and you will always be their prisoner.

LAO TZU

Chinese philosopher and writer.

6th-century BC

"Fearlessness presupposes calmness and peace of mind."

MAHATMA GANDHI

Anti-colonial nationalist and political ethicist,
who employed nonviolent resistance.

1869 - 1948

"The nearer a man comes to a calm mind, the closer he is to strength."

MARCUS AURELIUS

Roman emperor from 161 to 180 and a Stoic philosopher.

121 AD - 180 AD

"The mind freed from passions is an impenetrable fortress — a person has no more secure place of refuge for all time."

MARCUS AURELIUS

Roman emperor from 161 to 180 and a Stoic philosopher.

121 AD - 180 AD

"*Today I escaped from the crush of circumstances, or better put, I threw them out, for the crush wasn't from outside me but in my own assumptions.*"

MARCUS AURELIUS

Roman emperor from 161 to 180 and a Stoic philosopher.

121 AD - 180 AD

"Any person capable of angering you becomes your master."

_____

MARCUS AURELIUS

Roman emperor from 161 to 180 and a Stoic philosopher.

121 AD - 180 AD

"Misfortune can be minimized, but never eliminated. Life is full of seemingly endless trouble, and then life ends. Peace must be found in the imperfect present. "

MARCUS AURELIUS

Roman emperor from 161 to 180 and a Stoic philosopher.

121 AD - 180 AD

"Peace and quiet makes room for real contemplation. Contemplation allows the truth to emerge. Facing the truth would force us to transform. This is why we detest peace and quiet. This is why we sacrifice every quiet moment to trivial distraction."

MARCUS AURELIUS

Roman emperor from 161 to 180 and a Stoic philosopher.

121 AD - 180 AD

"Life is a storm that will test you unceasingly. Don't wait for calm waters that may not arrive. Derive purpose from resilience. Learn to sail the raging sea."

MARCUS AURELIUS

Roman emperor from 161 to 180 and a Stoic philosopher.

121 AD - 180 AD

"You have power over your mind – not outside events. Realize this, and you will find strength."

MARCUS AURELIUS

Roman emperor from 161 to 180 and a Stoic philosopher.

121 AD - 180 AD

"Everything turns on your assumptions about it, and that's on you. You can pluck out the hasty judgment at will, and like steering a ship around the point, you will find calm seas, fair weather and a safe port."

MARCUS AURELIUS

Roman emperor from 161 to 180 and a Stoic philosopher.

121 AD - 180 AD

"Anger is an acid that can do more harm to the vessel in which it is stored that anything on which it is poured."

MARK TWAIN

American writer, humorist, entrepreneur, publisher, and lecturer.

1835 - 1910

"If you do not conquer self, you will be conquered by self."

NAPOLEON HILL

American self-help author.

1883 - 1970

"The emotions of man are stirred more quickly than man's intelligence."

OSCAR WILDE

Irish poet and playwright.

1854 - 1900

"Fair peace becomes men; ferocious anger belongs to beasts."

OVID

Roman poet who lived during the reign of Augustus.

43 BC - 18AD

"When the mind is calm, how quickly, how smoothly, how beautifully you will perceive everything."

PARAMAHANSA YOGANANDA

Indian monk, yogi and guru.

1893 - 1952

"This too shall pass."

PERSIAN ADAGE

"He who is calm and happy nature will hardly feel the pressure of age, but to him who is of an opposite disposition youth and age are equally a burden."

PLATO

Athenian philosopher during the Classical period in Ancient Greece, founder of the Platonist school of thought.

428 BC - 347 BC

"Calm can solve all issues."

POPE SHENOUDA III

117th Pope of Alexandria and Patriarch of the
See of St. Mark.

1922 - 2012

"An angry man is again angry with himself when he returns to reason."

PUBLILIUS SYRUS

Latin writer, best known for his sententiae.

85 BC - 43 BC

"In the woods, we return to reason and faith. There I feel that nothing can befall me in life, — no disgrace, no calamity, (leaving me my eyes,) which nature cannot repair."

RALPH WALDO EMERSON

American essayist, lecturer, philosopher, and poet who led the transcendentalist movement of the mid-19th century.

1803 – 1882

"Nothing can bring you peace but yourself."

RALPH WALDO EMERSON

American essayist, lecturer, philosopher, and poet who led the transcendentalist movement of the mid-19th century.

1803 – 1882

"*Peace cannot be achieved through violence, it can only be attained through understanding.*"

RALPH WALDO EMERSON

American essayist, lecturer, philosopher, and poet who led the transcendentalist movement of the mid-19th century.

1803 – 1882

"God grant me the serenity to accept the things I cannot change, the courage to change the things I can, and the wisdom to the know the difference."

REINHOLD NIEBUHR

American Reformed theologian, ethicist and commentator.

1892 - 1971

*"Never be in a hurry;
do everything quietly
and in a calm spirit.
Do not lose your inner
peace for anything
whatsoever, even if
your whole world
seems upset."*

SAINT FRANCIS DE SALES

Bishop of Geneva and is honored as a saint in
the Catholic Church.

1567 - 1622

"No state is so bitter that a calm mind cannot find in it some consolation."

SENECA

Hispano-Roman Stoic philosopher, statesman and dramatist.

4 BC - 65 AD

"Accept what is necessary with a calm spirit. What happens that is new or beyond belief?"

SENECA

Hispano-Roman Stoic philosopher, statesman and dramatist.

4 BC - 65 AD

"Of all your troubles, great and small, the greatest are the ones that don't happen at all."

THOMAS CARLYLE

British historian, satirical writer, essayist, translator, philosopher, mathematician and teacher.

1795 - 1881

*"Nothing gives
one person so
much advantage over
another as to remain
always cool and
unruffled under all."
circumstances.*

THOMAS JEFFERSON

American statesman, diplomat, lawyer,
architect, philosopher, and Founding Father
who served as the third president of the United
States

1743 - 1826

"Few things are brought to a successful issue by impetuous desire, but most by calm and prudent forethought."

THUCYDIDES

Athenian historian and general.

460 BC - 400 BC

"In calmness lies true pleasure."

VICTOR HUGO

French poet, novelist, and dramatist of the
Romantic movement.

1802 - 1885

"Let's not forget that the little emotions are the great captains of our lives and we obey them without realizing it".

VINCENT VAN GOGH

Dutch post-impressionist painter who is among the most famous and influential figures in the history of Western art.

1853 - 1890

"The greatest weapon against stress is our ability to choose one thought over another."

WILLIAM JAMES

American philosopher and psychologist.

1842 - 1910

"When I look back on all these worries, I remember the story of the old man who said on his deathbed that he had had a lot of trouble in his life, most of which had never happened."

WINSTON CHURCHILL

British statesman, army officer, and writer. He was Prime Minister of the United Kingdom from 1940 to 1945 during the Second World War, and again from 1951 to 1955.

1874 - 1965

"Man conquers the world by conquering himself."

ZENO OF CITIUM

Hellenistic philosopher of Phoenician origin
from Citium, Cyprus

335 BC - 263 BC

"If we cannot end now our differences, at least we can help make the world safe for diversity. For, in the final analysis, our most basic common link is that we all inhabit this small planet. We all breathe the same air. We all cherish our children's future. And we are all mortal."

JOHN F. KENNEDY

35th United States President.

1917 - 1963

"It's not imagination on my part when I say that to look up at the sky, the clouds, the moon, and the stars make me calm and patient."

ANNE FRANK

German-born Dutch-Jewish diarist.

1929 - 1945

"Whatever is begun in anger, ends in shame."

Benjamin Franklin

American polymath and one of the Founding Fathers of the United States.

1706 - 1790

"*Anger is never without a reason, but seldom with a good one*".

BENJAMIN FRANKLIN

American polymath and one of the Founding
Fathers of the United States.

1706 - 1790

"Inner peace is beyond victory or defeat."

BHAGAVAD GITA

Sanskrit scripture that is part of the Hindu epic
Mahabharata.

Circa 400 BCE and 200 AD

"'Emotion can be the enemy, if you give into your emotion, you lose yourself. You must be at one with your emotions, because the body always follows the mind."

BRUCE LEE

Hong Kong-American actor, martial arts instructor, and philosopher

1940 -1973

"Those who act with few desires are calm, without worry or fear".

BUDDHA

Philosopher, teacher and religious leader on whose teachings Buddhism was founded.

563 BC - 483 BC

"Live in joy, in love,
even among those who hate.
Live in joy, in health,
even among the afflicted.
Live in joy, in peace,
even among the troubled.
Look within, be still.
Free from fear and attachment,
know the sweet joy of the way."

BUDDHA

Sage and philosopher on whose teachings
Buddhism was founded.

Circa 6th or 4th centuries BC

"A man who has not passed through the inferno of his passions, has never overcome them."

CARL JUNG

Carl Gustav Jung was a Swiss psychiatrist and psychoanalyst who founded analytical psychology.

1875 - 1961

"Tension is who you think you should be. Relaxation is who you are."

CHINESE PROVERB

"*If there is light in the soul, there will be beauty in the person. If there is beauty in the person, there will be harmony in the house. If there is harmony in the house, there will be order in the nation. If there is order in the nation, there will be peace in the world.*"

CHINESE PROVERB

"*If you are patient in one moment of anger, you will escape a hundred days of sorrow.*"

CHINESE PROVERB

"The gem cannot be polished without friction, nor man perfected without trial."

CONFUCIUS

Chinese philosopher and politician.

551 BC - 479 BC

"You wouldn't worry so much about what others think of you if you realized how seldom they do."

ELEANOR ROOSEVELT

American political figure, diplomat and activist.

1884 - 1962

"The chief task in life is simply this: to identify and separate matters so that I can say clearly to myself which are externals not under my control, and which have to do with the choices I actually control."

EPICTETUS

Greek Stoic philosopher.

Circa 55 – 135 AD

"When we are unable to find tranquility within ourselves, it is useless to seek it elsewhere."

FRANCOIS DE LA ROCHEFOUCAULD

French author of maxims and memoirs.

1613 - 1680

"Fear is the mind-killer."

FRANK HERBERT, DUNE

American science-fiction author

1920 - 1986

"He who cannot obey himself will be commanded. That is the nature of living creatures."

FRIEDRICH NIETZSCHE

German philosopher, essayist, and cultural critic.

1844 - 1900

"Fire in the heart, send smoke into the head."

GERMAN PROVERB

"The language of excitement is at best picturesque merely. You must be calm before you can utter oracles."

HENRY DAVID THOREAU

American naturalist, essayist, poet, and philosopher.

1817 - 1862

"There is nothing permanent except change."

HERACLITUS

Heraclitus of Ephesus was a pre-Socratic
Ionian Greek philosopher.

Circa 535 BC - 475 BC

"It is in changing that we find purpose."

HERACLITUS

Heraclitus of Ephesus was a pre-Socratic Ionian Greek philosopher.

Circa 535 BC - 475 BC

"Freedom from desire leads to inner peace."

LAO TSE

Chinese philosopher and writer.

6th-century BC

"Be content with what you have, rejoice in the way things are. When you realize there is nothing lacking, the whole world belongs to you."

LAO TZU

Chinese philosopher and writer.

6th-century BC

"Nothing is so aggravating as calmness."

MAHATMA GANDHI

Anti-colonial nationalist and political ethicist,
who employed nonviolent resistance.

1869 - 1948

"It is not the actions of others which trouble us (for those actions are controlled by their governing part), but rather it is our own judgments. Therefore, remove those judgments and resolve to let go of your anger, and it will already be gone. How do you let go? By realizing that such actions are not shameful to you."

MARCUS AURELIUS

Roman emperor from 161 to 180 and a Stoic philosopher.

121 AD - 180 AD

*"By going within.
Nowhere you can go is
more peaceful — more
free of interruptions —
than your own soul."*

MARCUS AURELIUS

Roman emperor from 161 to 180 and a Stoic
philosopher.

121 AD - 180 AD

"Short-term thinking makes people desperate, ungenerous, impulsive. Long-term thinking makes people calm, gracious, controlled."

MARCUS AURELIUS

Roman emperor from 161 to 180 and a Stoic philosopher.

121 AD - 180 AD

"Nowhere can man find a quieter or more untroubled retreat than in his own soul."

MARCUS AURELIUS

Roman emperor from 161 to 180 and a Stoic philosopher.

121 AD - 180 AD

"Stick with the situation at hand, and ask, "Why is this so unbearable? Why can't I endure it?" You'll be embarrassed to answer."

MARCUS AURELIUS

Roman emperor from 161 to 180 and a Stoic philosopher.

121 AD - 180 AD

"Like fragile ice, anger passes away in time"

OVID

Roman poet who lived during the reign of Augustus.

43 BC - 18AD

"The first and best victory is to conquer self. To be conquered by self is, of all things, the most shameful and vile."

PLATO

Athenian philosopher during the Classical period in Ancient Greece, founder of the Platonist school of thought.

428 BC - 347 BC

"There are two things a person should never be angry at, what they can help, and what they cannot."

PLATO

Athenian philosopher during the Classical period in Ancient Greece, founder of the Platonist school of thought.

428 BC - 347 BC

"Anger begins with folly, and ends in repentance."

PYTHAGORAS

Ancient Ionian Greek philosopher and the eponymous founder of Pythagoreanism.

569 BC - Died between 500 BC and 475 BC

"Change what cannot be accepted and accept what cannot be changed."

REINHOLD NIEBUHR

American Reformed theologian, ethicist and commentator.

1892 - 1971

"How does it help... to make troubles heavier by bemoaning them?"

SENECA

Hispano-Roman Stoic philosopher, statesman and dramatist.

4 BC - 65 AD

"Let us train our minds to desire what the situation demands."

SENECA

Hispano-Roman Stoic philosopher, statesman and dramatist.

4 BC - 65 AD

"Tact is the knack of making a point without making an enemy."

SIR ISAAC NEWTON

English mathematician, physicist, astronomer, theologian, and author who is widely recognised as one of the most influential scientists of all time and as a key figure in the scientific revolution.

1643 - 1727

"People won't have time for you if you are always angry or complaining."

***

STEPHEN HAWKING

English theoretical physicist, cosmologist and authour.

1942 - 2018

"Man should forget his anger before he lies down to sleep."

THOMAS DE QUINCEY

English essayist, best known for his
Confessions of an English Opium-Eater.

1785 - 1859

"The greatest remedy for anger is delay."

THOMAS PAINE

English-born American political activist.

1737 - 1809

"To be calm is the highest achievement of the self."

ZEN PROVERB

*"Night, the beloved.
Night, when words fade, and
things come alive. When the
destructive analysis of day
is done, and all that is truly
important becomes whole
and sound again. When man
reassembles his fragmentary
self and grows with the
calm of a tree."*

ANTOINE DE SAINT-EXUPERY

French writer, poet and pioneering aviator.

1900-1944

"Speak the truth,
do not yield to anger;
give, if thou art asked
for little; by these
three steps thou wilt
go near the gods."

CONFUCIUS

Chinese philosopher and politician.

551 BC - 479 BC

"Anger is one letter short of danger."

ELEANOR ROOSEVELT

American political figure, diplomat and activist.

1884 - 1962

"Some things are in our control and others not. Things in our control are opinion, pursuit, desire, aversion, and, in a word, whatever are our own actions."

EPICTETUS

Greek Stoic philosopher.

Circa 55 – 135 AD

"When people talk, listen completely. Most people never listen."

ERNEST HEMINGWAY

American journalist, novelist, short-story writer, and sportsman.

1899 - 1961

"The one who cannot restrain their anger will wish undone, what their temper and irritation prompted them to do."

HORACE

Roman lyric poet.

Circa 65 BC - 8 BC

"Observe things as they are and don't pay attention to other people. There are some people just like mad dogs barking at everything that moves, even barking when the wind stirs among the grass and leaves."

HUANG PO

Chinese master of Zen Buddhism.

Died circa 850

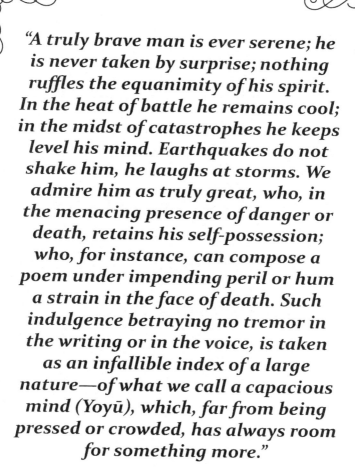

"*A truly brave man is ever serene; he is never taken by surprise; nothing ruffles the equanimity of his spirit. In the heat of battle he remains cool; in the midst of catastrophes he keeps level his mind. Earthquakes do not shake him, he laughs at storms. We admire him as truly great, who, in the menacing presence of danger or death, retains his self-possession; who, for instance, can compose a poem under impending peril or hum a strain in the face of death. Such indulgence betraying no tremor in the writing or in the voice, is taken as an infallible index of a large nature—of what we call a capacious mind (Yoyū), which, far from being pressed or crowded, has always room for something more.*"

INAZO NITOBE, BUSHIDO

Japanese agricultural economist, author, educator, diplomat, politician.

1862 - 1933

"The ideal of calm exists in a sitting cat."

JULES RENARD

French writer.

1864 – 1910

"*Life is a series of natural and spontaneous changes. Don't resist them; that only creates sorrow. Let reality be reality. Let things flow naturally forward in whatever way they like.*"

LAO TZU

Chinese philosopher and writer.

6th-century BC

"He who is contented is rich."

LAO TZU

Chinese philosopher and writer.

6th-century BC

"The way to do is to be."

LAO TZU

Chinese philosopher and writer.

6th-century BC

"Rushing into action, you fail. Trying to grasp things, you lose them. Forcing a project to completion, you ruin what was almost ripe. Therefore, the Master takes action by letting things take their course. He remains as calm at the end as at the beginning. He has nothing, thus has nothing to lose. What he desires is non-desire; what he learns is to unlearn. He simply reminds people of who they have always been. He cares about nothing but the Tao. Thus, he can care for all things."

LAO TZU

Chinese philosopher and writer.

6th-century BC

"Whoever is in a hurry shows that the thing he is about is too big for him."

LORD CHESTERFIELD

4th Earl of Chesterfield, KG, PC was a British statesman, diplomat, man of letters.

1694 - 1773

"In a gentle way, you can shake the world."

MAHATMA GANDHI

Anti-colonial nationalist and political ethicist, who employed nonviolent resistance.

1869 - 1948

"The best vaccine against anger is to watch others in its throes."

MARCEL PROUST

French novelist, critic, and essayist.

1871 - 1922

"Receive without pride, let go without attachment."

MARCUS AURELIUS

Roman emperor from 161 to 180 and a Stoic philosopher.

121 AD - 180 AD

"Don't set your mind on things you don't possess as if they were yours, but count the blessings you actually possess and think how much you would desire them if they weren't already yours. "

MARCUS AURELIUS

Roman emperor from 161 to 180 and a Stoic philosopher.

121 AD - 180 AD

"At every moment keep a sturdy mind on the task at hand, as a Roman and human being, doing it with strict and simple dignity, affection, freedom, and justice — giving yourself a break from all other considerations. You can do this if you approach each task as if it is your last, giving up every distraction, emotional subversion of reason, and all drama, vanity, and complaint over your fair share. You can see how mastery over a few things makes it possible to live an abundant and devout life — for, if you keep watch over these things, the gods won't ask for more."

MARCUS AURELIUS

Roman emperor from 161 to 180 and a Stoic philosopher.

121 AD - 180 AD

"Discard your misperceptions. Stop being jerked like a puppet. Limit yourself to the present."

MARCUS AURELIUS

Roman emperor from 161 to 180 and a Stoic philosopher.

121 AD - 180 AD

"A wise man never loses anything, if he has himself."

MICHEL DE MONTAIGNE

Philosopher of the French Renaissance.

1533 - 1592

"A smile is the beginning of peace."

MOTHER TERESA

Roman Catholic nun and missionary honored
in the Catholic Church as Saint Teresa
of Calcutta.

1910 - 1997

"How you can sit there, calmly eating muffins when we are in this horrible trouble, I can't make out. You seem to me to be perfectly heartless."

"Well, I can't eat muffins in an agitated manner. The butter would probably get on my cuffs. One should always eat muffins quite calmly. It is the only way to eat them."

OSCAR WILDE, THE IMPORTANCE OF BEING EARNEST

Irish poet and playwright. One of the most popular playwrights in 1880's London.

1854 - 1900

*"Learn silence.
With the quiet serenity
of a meditative
mind, listen, absorb,
transcribe, and
transform."*

PYTHAGORAS

Ancient Ionian Greek philosopher and the
eponymous founder of Pythagoreanism.

**569 BC - Died between 500 BC
and 475 BC**

"Great events make me quiet and calm; it is only the trifles that irritate my nerves."

QUEEN VICTORIA

Queen of the United Kingdom of Great Britain and Ireland from 20 June 1837 until 1901. Known as the Victorian era.

1837 - 1901

"Nothing external to you has any power over you."

RALPH WALDO EMERSON

American essayist, lecturer, philosopher, and poet who led the transcendentalist movement of the mid-19th century.

1803 – 1882

"If the blood humor is too strong and robust, calm it with balance and harmony."

XUN KUANG

Chinese Confucian philosopher and writer who lived during the Warring States period.

310 BC - 235 BC

"A calm and modest life
brings more happiness
than the pursuit of
success combined with
constant restlessness."

ALBERT EINSTEIN

German-born theoretical physicist who
developed the theory of relativity.

1979 - 1955

"*Peace comes from within. Do not seek it without.*"

BUDDHA

Sage and philosopher on whose teachings
Buddhism was founded.

Circa 6th or 4th centuries BC

"Do not learn how to react. Learn how to respond."

BUDDHA

Sage and philosopher on whose teachings
Buddhism was founded.

Circa 6th or 4th centuries BC

"Holding on to anger is like grasping a hot coal with the intent of throwing it at someone else; you are the one who gets burned."

BUDDHA

Sage and philosopher on whose teachings
Buddhism was founded.

Circa 6th or 4th centuries BC

"Chase after money and security and your heart will never unclench. Care about people's approval and you will be their prisoner. Do your work, then step back. The only path to serenity."

LAO TZU

Chinese philosopher and writer.

6th-century BC

Printed in Great Britain
by Amazon